Ellen Doris

Life at the Top

Discoveries in a Tropical Forest Canopy

STECK-VAUGHN
ELEMENTARY · SECONDARY · ADULT · LIBRARY

A Harcourt Company

www.steck-vaughn.com

For Michael John and Working Man John,
true fans of the canopy crane

Steck-Vaughn Company

First published 2001 by Raintree Steck-Vaughn Publishers,
an imprint of Steck-Vaughn Company.

Copyright © 2001 Turnstone Publishing Group, Inc.
Copyright © 2000, text, by Ellen Doris.

ISBN 0-7398-2480-5

For information about this and other Turnstone reference books and educational materials, visit Turnstone Publishing Group on the World Wide Web at http://www.turnstonepub.com.

Photo and illustration credits listed on page 48 constitute part of this copyright page.

Printed and bound in the United States of America.

1 2 3 4 5 6 7 8 9 0 LB 05 04 03 02 01 00

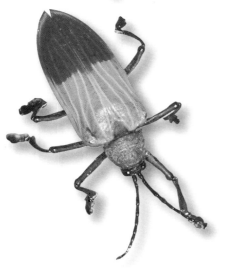

Contents

1 The Canopy

At the top of a tree as tall as a ten-story building, an iguana as big as a full-grown cat stretches out to soak up the sun. The iguana lives in Metropolitan Natural Park, just outside of Panama City, Panama. Here there are trees with trunks so thick that three to four people holding hands could just reach around them. Climbing plants called **lianas** (pronounced lee-AH-nas) wind around the tree trunks and branches. Mosses and other plants grow on their bark. High in the treetops, sloths creep in slow motion. Brightly colored butterflies drink juice from rotting fruit.

The forest in Metropolitan Natural Park is about 80 years old. It's on land where people once cut down all the trees.

Panama City

The forest in Metropolitan Natural Park is a **tropical forest**. That means it is near the **equator**, in the **tropics**. Tropical forests are home to an amazing number of plants and animals. More than half of the species that scientists have identified live in tropical forests. A **species** is one of the groups used by scientists to **classify**, or group, living things. Animals of the same species are able to mate with one another and give birth to young that can also breed and produce young.

Katydid

Sloth

Iguana

Vulture

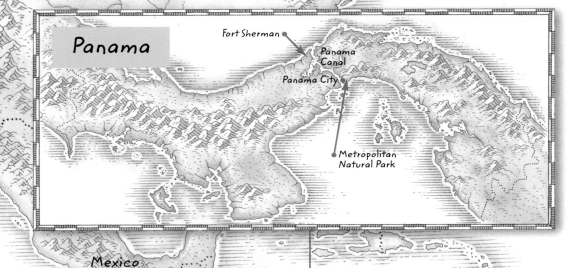

United States of America

ATLANTIC OCEAN

Panama

Fort Sherman

Panama Canal

Panama City

Metropolitan Natural Park

Mexico

Caribbean Sea

Finding the Forests

There are different kinds of tropical forests in Panama. Scientists at the Smithsonian Tropical Research Institute (STRI) often work in the **rain forest** at Fort Sherman and the **dry tropical forest** at Metropolitan Natural Park.

Rain Forest

In rain forests there is often heavy rain. More species live in rain forests than in most other places in the world.

Fort Sherman

Dry Tropical Forest

Dry tropical forests have a rainy season and a dry season. These forests have fewer species than rain forests.

Metropolitan Natural Park

South America

N

PACIFIC OCEAN

Each year many new species of plants and animals are found in tropical forests. Although these forests cover only about 14 percent of the land on Earth, more than half of the world's species may live in these special places. At the Smithsonian Tropical Research Institute (called STRI for short), scientists study tropical forests. Metropolitan Natural Park is one of the main places where they do research.

Annette Aiello has studied Panama's forest insects for 20 years. Still, this STRI scientist keeps finding species that she has never seen before. "It's amazing," she says.

Life at the Top

The trees and other plants that grow in a forest form layers. One of the top layers is called the **canopy**. It is made of the branching tops of tall trees. In tropical forests, canopy branches are often draped with lianas. They may also be covered with epiphytes. Epiphytes are plants that grow on other plants instead of growing in the ground. Seen from an airplane, the leaves of canopy trees, lianas, and epiphytes look like a bumpy, green carpet.

The canopy of a tropical forest is full of life. Most of the leaves that grow in the forest are up in the canopy. That lets them get a lot of sunlight. All those leaves attract crowds of beetles, caterpillars, and other leaf-eating animals. Birds, lizards, and spiders come to eat the leaf-eaters. In turn, other animals come to eat the birds, lizards, and spiders. Thousands of species can be found in tropical treetops.

Forest Layers

Forest layers aren't neatly divided. They cross over each other. But layers help scientists describe the life found in a forest and its living conditions.

Spider

Lizard

Royal Flycatcher bird

Katydid

Snake

Iguana

Praying mantis

Silky Anteater

Sloth

Liana

Bromeliad flower

Emergent Layer

The extra-tall trees that poke out above the canopy form the emergent layer. This layer gets lots of sun and wind.

Canopy Layer

This layer is made of the branching tops of tall trees. Like a roof, this layer is open to wind and sun. It can rise as tall as 60 meters (about 200 feet).

Most of the life in a tropical forest can be found in the canopy. Spiders, lizards, birds, praying mantises, iguanas, anteaters, sloths, snakes, katydids, flowers, and lianas are common sights in many tropical canopies.

Understory Layer

Young canopy trees, palms, and adult understory trees grow here. The air is still and humid in the understory and lower layers. The temperature doesn't change much.

Shrub Layer

Woody shrubs are found here.

Ground Layer

Herbs, small ferns, young trees, lianas, and young palm plants grow here. This is the darkest layer in the forest.

9

Biodiversity Around the Globe

Scientists don't know the exact number of species on Earth. But they do know that the greatest number of plant and animal species are in the tropics. And in the tropics, the places with the greatest biodiversity are near the equator. The equator is an imaginary line that divides north from south on the globe. In general, biodiversity decreases as you move north or south of the equator.

In one study, scientists found 56 species of breeding birds in Greenland, which is in the Arctic. New York State had 195. Guatemala had 469 species, and Panama had 1,100. Colombia, which is near the equator, had 1,395. That's almost 25 times more species of breeding birds in Colombia than in Greenland. Why? Scientists aren't sure. Some think it has something to do with the amount of rain in the tropics and the steady warm temperatures. Scientists are studying places like tropical forests to see if this idea is right.

Biodiversity

Scientists use the word **biodiversity** to talk about the different kinds of plants and animals found in a particular place. The more species there are, the greater the biodiversity. Biodiversity is important because one species often depends on other species to live. The loss of one species could lead to the extinction, or death, of another.

Scientists study biodiversity in many different ways. They may count the number of species found in one place. Or they may count to see how many of one species they can find. They also may look at the different ways plants and animals live with each other and their surroundings.

Earth's biodiversity is greatest in the tropics, especially in the forests. Within the forests, the canopy is the place with the largest number of species.

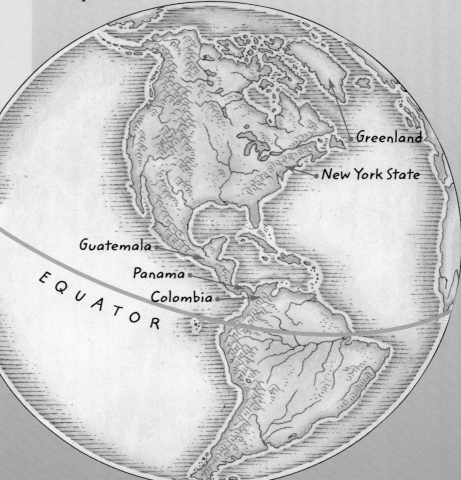

There can be a lot of differences even in one forest layer. The top of the canopy can be a hot, dry, windy place. Just a little lower down in the layer, it can be cooler, more humid, and still. STRI scientist Yves Basset says, "There may be another world to be discovered in the canopy's surface."

Lots to Learn

Americans and Europeans who explored tropical forests in the 1800s were surprised at the many different kinds of plants and animals they saw. In the forests near their homes, they were used to seeing about 25 different species of trees. But some tropical forests they visited had 200 or 300 tree species. One 19th-century explorer, Alfred Russel Wallace, said that "if the traveler notices a particular species and wishes to find more like it, he may often turn his eyes in vain in every direction." Trees of different sizes, shapes, and colors are all around him, "but he rarely sees any one of them repeated." The many kinds of life in tropical forests still interest scientists today.

Scientists are especially fascinated by all the different kinds of life in the canopy. The canopy is full of plants and animals, yet most of them are not well known. The canopy holds many secrets for scientists to find out about. How do animals in the canopy live? Where do different species travel to find food? What do they eat? What eats them?

"The canopy is a mystery," says Elroy Charles, a scientist who studies tropical beetles at STRI. "I suppose that's why so many scientists want to study it. They want to know what's going on. There is a lot still unanswered."

In 1990 the United Nations Environment Programme and STRI started the Tropical Forest Canopy Programme. This project has brought many scientists up into the canopy of Metropolitan Natural Park. What they learn there can help us understand how tropical forests came to have so many kinds of plants and animals. It may also show us what keeps them that way so that we can conserve, or protect, their biodiversity.

Alfred Russel Wallace (1823–1913) explored South America. He collected samples for more than four years. Sadly, these were all lost in a fire. But Wallace wrote the story of his time in Brazil in *Travels on the Amazon and Rio Negro*. The book is still read by tropical scientists today.

Scientists like Elroy Charles spend many hours in tropical forests trying to find out more about all the animals and plants there. Here Elroy is collecting insects to study.

2 Getting off the Ground

Scientists like Hector Barrios can easily study the lowest layers of tropical forests. Farther up, it's not so easy.

For more than 100 years, scientists have wondered about the diversity, or different kinds, of life in tropical forest canopies. Much of that life still is not well understood, partly because the canopy is not easy to reach. Some of the trees are taller than ten-story buildings, and reaching their branches is difficult. Scientists who do make it up may face stinging insects, poisonous snakes, driving rain, or high winds. Scientists have tried to find safe, easy ways to get up into the canopy.

In 1958 a tower was built in a tropical forest near Kampala, Uganda, in Africa. It is still there. Anyone willing to climb 35 meters (about 120 feet) can get a great view of the forest canopy. Since then, towers have been built in many other forests.

Much can be seen from a tower. It is perfect for someone who wants to watch a bird's nest for many hours in a day. But scientists wanted a way to move around in the canopy. Since the 1960s, sky-high walkways have been built in several forest canopies. Walkways let scientists travel easily from tree to tree. Unfortunately, walkways take a long time to build.

Some scientists climb tropical trees using ropes and gear invented for mountain climbing. Scientists can use them to study many different parts of a forest. Climbing is fun, but it can also be dangerous and slow. It isn't the best choice for someone who needs to check many different places in one day.

The canopy raft, used since 1989, might be the most unusual way to get to the top of a forest. The raft is made of nets stretched between large floats. It is carried above the canopy by a big, colorful blimp, or airship. The blimp then places the raft on top of the trees. This makes a surface that scientists can sit or walk on.

(left)
Scientist Philip Wittman is on a canopy walkway in Peru.

(below)
Scientist Meg Lowman, who studies plants at the Marie Selby Botanical Garden in Sarasota, Florida, is climbing into the canopy.

The Canopy Raft System was invented by French scientist Francis Hallé. It has been used in many different tropical forests.

(above)
This is the crane in Metropolitan Natural Park.

(inset)
Alan Smith of STRI (left) and Geoffrey Parker of the Smithsonian Environmental Research Center reach for a canopy leaf. It was Alan's idea to place cranes in tropical forests.

Gliding Through the Treetops

In the late 1980s, a STRI scientist named Alan Smith had a new idea. Why not put a crane in the forest? Cranes can lift heavy objects high into the air. Maybe one could carry scientists up into the trees. Alan's idea came to be in 1990, when the world's very first "canopy crane" was placed in Panama's Metropolitan Natural Park.

The crane's 42-meter (about 140-foot) tower is taller than the trees. The crane has a long arm, about 51 meters (170 feet) in length. A small metal cage, called a **gondola**, dangles from the arm. It holds the scientists and their equipment. The crane's operator can move the gondola up and down like an elevator. The operator can swing the crane's arm along a big curved path so that the gondola can move over a very large area.

The crane makes it easy to get information that was once difficult or impossible to collect. For example, scientists learn about the habits of insects by watching them from the gondola. They also use machines that measure gases in the air and in the leaves to study how trees take in gases. The crane can bring the machines to the top of the canopy.

Plus, it is exciting to "fly" up to the tops of the trees and to glide among all the beautiful plants and interesting forest creatures that live there. Says STRI scientist Annette Aiello, who has taken many rides in the gondola, "If you're afraid of heights, you may have a problem going up. But when you get there, you'll find it's like a green carpet that you wish you could step out onto."

Choosing a Way Up

What's the best way to get to the canopy? It may depend on the type of questions the scientist wants to answer. But scientists are also very practical people. Often they design their experiments based on what they have to work with. That may be a tower, a walkway, a crane, or a set of ropes.

In 1997 STRI put up a second crane near Fort Sherman in Panama. The two cranes let scientists compare the information they collect in the rain forest at Fort Sherman and the dry tropical forest of Metropolitan Natural Park. There are also canopy cranes in other places around the world, including Venezuela, the United States, Australia, Japan, Switzerland, and Malaysia.

Up, Up, and Away—
How the Canopy Crane Works

The tower of the crane at Metropolitan Natural Park is 42 meters (about 140 feet) high. The crane's arm can travel in a full circle, 102 meters (about 340 feet) wide. The gondola, or metal cage, moves along the arm on a trolley and moves up and down with a pulley.

This gondola is big enough to carry three people and their equipment.

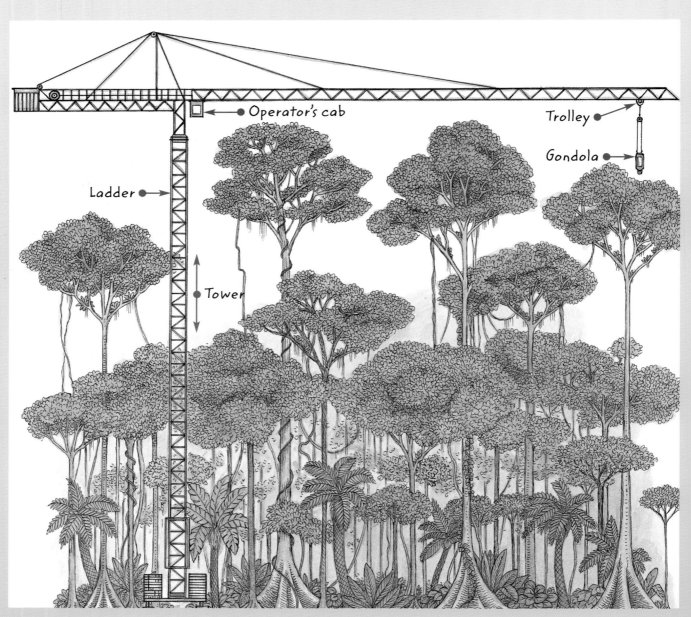

Operator's cab

Trolley

Gondola

Ladder

Tower

1 Oscard Saldaña, the crane operator, has to climb a ladder inside the crane tower to get up to the cab where the controls are. Once he is in the cab, he signals to the scientists to get in the gondola.

2 Scientists Vojtech Novotny and Hector Barrios prepare the gondola for a ride up into the canopy. Hector then gets in, shuts the door, and lets the operator know that he's ready to go up. He uses walkie-talkies and hand signals to talk with and signal to the operator.

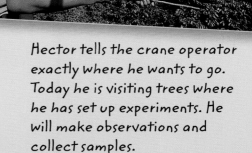

3 Hector tells the crane operator exactly where he wants to go. Today he is visiting trees where he has set up experiments. He will make observations and collect samples.

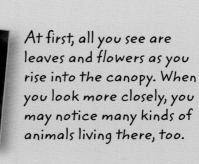

At first, all you see are leaves and flowers as you rise into the canopy. When you look more closely, you may notice many kinds of animals living there, too.

3 What's There?

The canopy holds thousands and thousands of different kinds of insects. These are just a few.

The canopy of a tropical forest is a treasure trove for **entomologists**, the scientists who study insects. It's full of "bugs." Entomologists want to know which insects live in tropical canopies. They also want to know how many different species there are and whether each is rare or common. To do this, they collect insects from the canopy.

There are lots of ways to catch insects. You can net them, trap them, dig them out of soil, or wash them from plants. Scientists have different ways to catch different kinds of insects. For example, many night-flying moths and beetles are drawn to light. Special traps with lights are used to collect them. But mosquitoes aren't drawn to light, and few end up in light traps. Scientists have to find just the right way to catch the insects they want to study.

The smallest insect shown here is this long: ⊢—⊣. The largest insect is this long: ⊢————————⊣.

Gall Makers and Leaf Miners

Hector Barrios teaches students who want to be entomologists. The students learn how to study insects by doing research with him. Recently, Hector and two students, Anayansi Valderrama and Enrique Medianero, used STRI's canopy cranes to look for insects. They wanted to compare the insects in Metropolitan Natural Park with those at Fort Sherman. They also wanted to compare insects living in different layers of the same forest.

The students studied a group of insects called **gall makers**. Most gall makers are flies, but some are wasps or other insects. They aren't all closely related, but they all use forest plants in the same way. They make parts of the plant swell, or grow larger. These swellings, called **galls**, form on a leaf or stem. It happens like this. An insect lays an egg on a plant. The chemicals she puts near the egg make the leaf or stem swell. This makes a kind of "room" for the young insect, where it will develop into an adult.

Hector is carefully checking canopy leaves for galls. If you cut open a gall, you can see the insect "room" inside.

Hector and his students looked for **leaf miners**, too. These insects tunnel through the soft insides of leaves. Most leaf miners are the **larvae**, or young, of moths. The larvae of some flies, wasps, and beetles are miners, too. Miners grow as they tunnel through leaves. Some chew their way out before they are fully grown, but others stay inside until they are ready to turn into adults. Different kinds of leaf miners make differently shaped tunnels. Some tunnels are straight, while others look like ragged spots. Still others twist and turn.

Gall-making and leaf-mining larvae do not move around a lot, so they are easy to collect by hand. Of course, scientists have to find them first. Hector, Anayansi, and Enrique did this by looking closely at leaves as they traveled around in the crane's gondola. Whenever they spotted a leaf with a gall or a mine, they picked it. Often the larvae were still inside. They collected empty galls and mines, too, because these could tell them about the insects that once lived inside.

These tunnels were made by leaf miners. The insect that made each tunnel may still be inside the leaf.

Galling Mysteries

It's easy to know what kind of insect lived inside this gall from Colorado. You can see the new adult gall midge standing by part of its pupal case, or the case that held it while it was developing. But in the tropics, scientists usually can't match galls to adult insects. They can cut galls open and find out what type of larva is inside. But in most cases, scientists don't know which insect larva grows into which adult insect. It's a mystery.

Galls are found in many places. Different kinds of gall wasps and gall flies like the one above live in many

different countries. And each kind of wasp or fly makes a different gall. Scientists think that the tropical galls on the top left were made by the larvae of a tiny fly called a gall midge. But they aren't sure yet what insects made the other galls. They will have to watch each gall when a new adult comes out and identify the insect to solve the mystery.

Hector and the students put each leaf into a clear bag and marked the bags so they could remember when and where they found each sample. They kept track of all this information. Without it they couldn't compare the different areas they had questions about.

Surprising Results

"At the beginning," Hector says, "we thought that maybe different species lived in each area of a forest because they were adapted to different conditions." But they also thought that many insects would live in more than one part of the forest. The insects they collected surprised them. "Most of the species in the canopy are found only in the canopy. Most of the species in the understory are only in the understory," Hector explains.

The scientists found only two kinds of gall makers that live in both the canopy and the understory layers of Metropolitan Natural Park. At Fort Sherman they found only one kind of gall maker living in both layers.

Not many insects live in both forests, either. Only one gall-making species was found living in both places. Probably

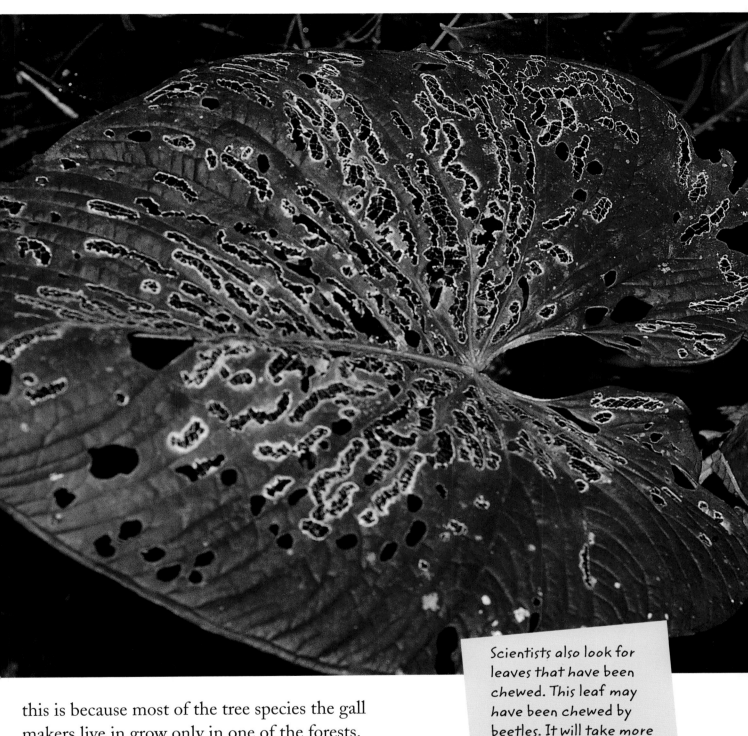

this is because most of the tree species the gall makers live in grow only in one of the forests. The results were almost the same for leaf miners. This surprise made Hector and his students appreciate the differences between the two tropical forests. It also helped them understand more about biodiversity within a forest.

Scientists also look for leaves that have been chewed. This leaf may have been chewed by beetles. It will take more collecting work before scientists can know for certain.

Sampling

No one can catch and count every single insect in a forest, or even in one tree. So scientists collect samples from different parts of the area they want to study.

They use the samples to test their ideas about the whole area. For this to work, they need many samples.

That's why Elroy samples 40 different branches in both the canopy and the understory each time he collects. Elroy plans to collect samples every week for eight months. Here Elroy uses a beating tray. The other trap has clear sides to catch flying beetles.

Hunting Beetles

Elroy Charles is interested in a family of beetles called **chrysomelids** (pronounced kris-o-MEL-ids), or leaf beetles. Some of them are beautiful, with shiny metallic colors. Elroy thinks that leaf beetles are some of the most interesting insects around.

Elroy has a lot of questions about chrysomelids. He wants to know exactly where each kind lives and what it eats. He also wonders how chrysomelids affect forest plants. To answer these questions, he collects canopy and understory beetles at Metropolitan Natural Park and Fort Sherman.

Gall-making and leaf-mining larvae stay in one place, but leaf beetles move around. This is one of the reasons that Elroy collects them in several ways. If he collected only by hand, he might overlook beetles that crawl under leaves or fly away. Certain traps will catch flying beetles but miss those that are sitting still. By using different ways to catch beetles, Elroy hopes to capture more of them. This will help him get more of the information he wants.

One method Elroy uses is hand collecting. He looks closely at leaves. If he spots a beetle, he grabs it. After Elroy catches what he can by hand, he "beats" for insects. First, he holds a large, flat beating tray under a branch. Then, he hits the branch with a stick. A few insects may hold onto the branch, but others fall into the tray. He scoops these up and puts them in a container. He tries to work quickly, so not too many fly away.

Elroy also tries to trap beetles. One kind of trap hangs from a branch and catches beetles as they fly through the air. It has a clear back. If flying beetles don't notice the trap, they crash into it and fall, stunned, into a container below.

Another kind of trap catches chrysomelids that live underground as larvae. Elroy puts these traps near tree roots. He hopes to catch the new adults when they crawl out and fly away. Elroy isn't sure how well the traps will work. He wants to try them, though, because he knows that hand collecting and beating won't catch beetles that are flying. If the traps don't collect many beetles, Elroy will move them to a new place to see if they catch more there.

Hector helps Elroy. Here Hector is setting up a net to collect insects. The net hangs down to the ground like a tent. Hector hopes it will catch new adult chrysomelids as they fly up from the ground.

Elroy keeps a set of information sheets. He writes down what he collects, when he collects it, and where he finds it. The sheets can help scientists understand more about how insects live.

Hector and Elroy also attach a tag to each of the trees they sample. The tags will help them find the trees again. The numbers and letters for each tree are recorded on information sheets.

Beetles aren't the only thing Elroy collects. He also gathers information about the trees where he finds the beetles. This may help him figure out what the beetles are eating. He looks carefully at leaves because he can tell by the holes or scraped places which kind of beetle was feeding. Chewed leaves suggest the number of beetles in an area, too. The more leaf damage there is, the more beetles there are in the area. Elroy also estimates how many of the leaves on each tree are new. New leaves are easier for chrysomelids to chew. And he notes if the tree has flowers, because some beetles feed on them.

Scientists think that most tropical insects can only live in certain places. Some may eat only the leaves of one kind of vine. Others may be able to live in only one forest layer. Elroy's studies of leaf beetles will help scientists decide if some of their ideas about tropical insects are right.

What will Elroy collect in his traps? "I don't know," he says. "It's a surprise." Tropical forests are full of insects no one has ever seen before.

4 Back on the Ground

A scientist can collect enough insects in one day to stay busy in the lab for weeks or even months. "Sometimes I sleep and dream that I'm putting a beetle in a glass bottle," says Elroy.

Collecting insects or information in the canopy is just the beginning of a scientist's job. Once this work is done, the long hours in the lab begin. Scientists may need to identify an unknown insect or offer it different leaves to see what it eats. They also must organize and review their notes and other information. They have to look carefully through their information and search for patterns.

In some places scientists recognize most of the plants and animals they find. That's not the case in tropical canopies. There are so many species, and so few are well known, that "new" species turn up all the time. Of course, the plants and animals themselves aren't really new. But they are new to scientists, who are seeing, describing, and naming them for the first time.

You might not think it would matter much to Elroy Charles if the beetles he finds have names or not. After all, names won't change where the beetles go or what they eat, and that's what Elroy is interested in. Even so, it's a lot easier for scientists to study insects that have names. Scientists want to learn from one another. They also want to share their results, so they need to know when they are talking about the same kind of beetle.

Names help scientists talk with each other and share information, but there are more reasons for naming. When scientists name a new plant or animal, they do more than just decide what to call it. They try to figure out what other species it is most like. They group it with others that share important features. Understanding these likenesses can be useful.

(above)
Once he's identified an insect, Elroy puts it into a collection with similar insects. These collections can help him identify new insects.

(below)
Scientists like Elroy (left) and Yves Basset sometimes use computers to help them compare the insects they find to other insects.

Each week Elroy looks over the leaf beetles he has collected. "This is where the work becomes very difficult," he says. He sometimes collects more than 200 beetles. He often spots a kind he hasn't seen before. When this happens, he looks closely to see if it is like any of the chrysomelid groups he knows. Do its hind legs look puffed up? It might be a new kind of jumping flea beetle. Do its sides stick out so that it looks like it has a shell? Perhaps it belongs with the tortoise beetle group.

At this point Elroy sends one of the new beetles to a special entomologist who is an expert on chrysomelids. More than 30,000 species of chrysomelids have already been named, so often it takes an expert to identify a beetle. The entomologist compares the beetle to others in her or his collection. If the beetle is new, the entomologist and Elroy might write a paper describing what it looks like and anything else they know about it. They will give it a name, too. This helps other scientists identify chrysomelids they find.

It isn't enough for Elroy to name the beetles he finds. He wants to know what each species eats, too, so he runs feeding experiments. He offers each beetle a piece of a leaf from the place where the beetle was found. If the beetle eats the leaf, Elroy has discovered at least one of its food plants. If it doesn't, even after a few days, then it probably eats something else. Feeding experiments help Elroy tell whether insects he collected were actually eating the plants they were found on or just passing through.

When Elroy collects insects, he takes a few of the nearby leaves, too. He uses the leaves he's collected to see what the beetles eat. He picks young leaves because most leaf beetles are small and they can only eat young, tender leaves. He offers a bit of leaf to each beetle.

What Will It Be?

Annette Aiello is an entomologist with a talent for raising insects. Other scientists are always dropping by with insect eggs and larvae that they would like to know more about. Annette puts the tiny ones into small dishes. Larger ones might go into small, screened cages or empty soft drink bottles. After the insects settle in, she watches to see what happens.

Once a scientist brought Annette an old bird's nest he had found. Two small, gray larvae were living inside. If Annette moved suddenly, they dived down into the nest.

Most people don't like it when insects come into their homes. But Annette Aiello thinks that the insects on her kitchen wall are as interesting as the ones outside, or in her lab. Sometimes a lizard runs over and gobbles up the insect she's watching. "I know the lizards need to eat," says Annette, "but that can be a bother."

But if she watched quietly for a while, they came out and started eating the lining of the nest. Annette knew that the larvae would grow up into beetles. The shape of their soft bodies, their hard heads, and their chewing mouth parts gave that much away. But she didn't know what kind of beetles the larvae would become.

Annette decided to raise the larvae until they turned into adults. Maybe the adults would be familiar to her or to another entomologist. If the adults were unfamiliar, she would send them to a beetle expert who would describe and name them. In either case, her information would help scientists identify other beetles like these and understand how they live.

First, Annette folded a piece of window screen. She sewed the edges shut to make a cage for the nest so the larvae couldn't escape. Then, she hung her homemade cage in a screened greenhouse.

Annette tried to save everything when she raised two mystery larvae. Below is an adult beetle that came out of the cocoon, or outer covering, that the larva made from the nest material.

34

A spray of water showered the nest four times a day so that it would stay damp. The breeze passing through the cage helped prevent mold, the way it would if the nest were still in the forest. Annette wanted the larvae to grow up, so the conditions in the greenhouse had to match the conditions the larvae were used to.

During the days that followed, the larvae continued to live in and eat the lining of the nest. Annette observed them regularly, recording what she noticed. One week later, one of the larvae stopped eating. It surrounded itself with bits of nest material, making a ball-shaped cocoon, or covering. Another week went by, and the second larva made a cocoon, too.

Annette knew that inside their cocoons the larvae were gradually changing. If all went well, she would soon be able to see what the adult beetles looked like. Annette watched patiently for more than two weeks. Finally, a small, dark-colored beetle broke out of the first cocoon. The second beetle appeared four days later.

The beetles had what looked like little balls on their antennae. The balls could open up like a hand with flat fingers. This convinced Annette that they belonged to a large group called scarab beetles. But she hadn't seen this particular kind before.

Annette wrote to Jan Krikken, an entomologist in Holland, for help. A few years earlier, Jan had written about and made drawings of a new scarab beetle. He named it *Genuchinus muzo*. A close look at the beetles Annette raised made Jan sure that her beetles belonged to the same species. Now, thanks to Annette, all the stages of the insect's life are known.

Who Am I?

A scientist follows a series of steps to identify an insect. Annette and other scientists take each step in order.

First, the scientist looks carefully at the insect to see if it is familiar. Then,

❶ if it's unfamiliar, the scientist tries to get help from books, collections, and other scientists.

❷ if the insect isn't in any books, the scientist sends it away to an expert.

❸ if the expert can't identify it, the scientist announces the discovery of a new insect. This beetle is a *Phyllophaga*.

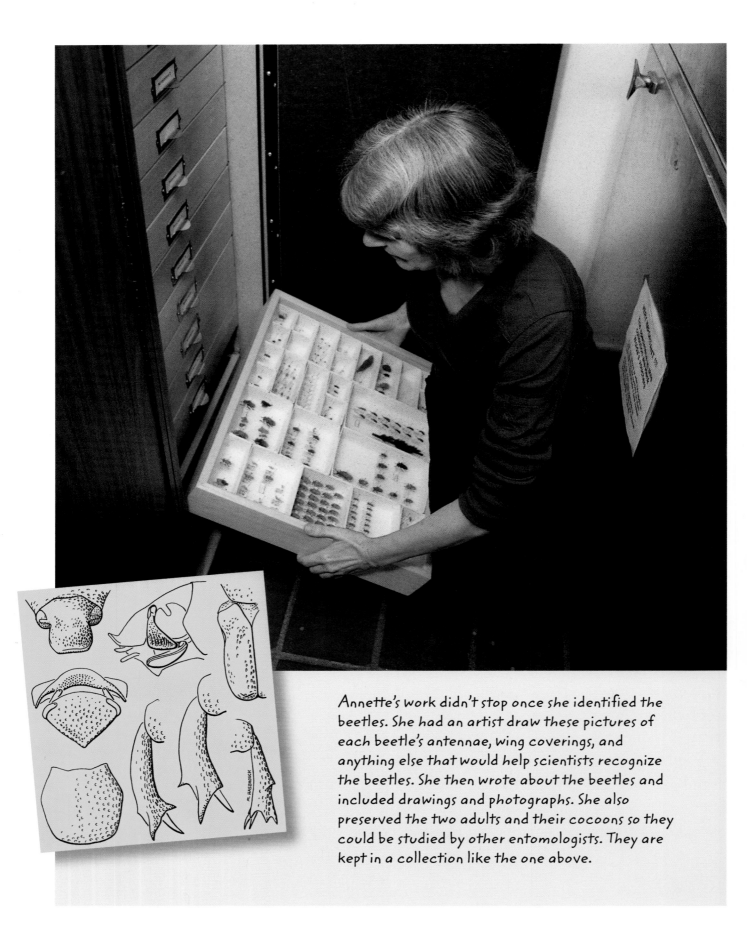

Annette's work didn't stop once she identified the beetles. She had an artist draw these pictures of each beetle's antennae, wing coverings, and anything else that would help scientists recognize the beetles. She then wrote about the beetles and included drawings and photographs. She also preserved the two adults and their cocoons so they could be studied by other entomologists. They are kept in a collection like the one above.

Keeping Records

Annette keeps careful records about every insect she raises. She notes when and where each was collected, what it ate, and when it stopped eating. "I keep track of everything they do," Annette explains, "and I save all the parts." These parts include empty eggshells, shed caterpillar skins, empty cocoons, and the preserved adult insects. All the parts are marked and added to her collection. This collection is used by Annette, other scientists, and students who want to learn about insects.

Annette is interested in taxonomy, or grouping species. **Taxonomists** try to understand which insects are most alike. Then, they can group them in ways that show the likenesses. Raising insects and keeping careful track of what they do and what they look like are important parts of Annette's work. Knowing more about how insects are related can help scientists understand more about biodiversity, or the different kinds of life here on Earth.

Annette stores her insects in collections. The trays below are part of her butterfly collection. The butterflies in each tray are grouped by species. That makes it easier to find a sample later if Annette needs it to identify a new insect.

5 Connections

The strawberry poison-dart frog is tiny, only about two centimeters (about 3/4 inch) long. But this frog is safe from many animals that would eat it because it can produce a strong poison. The frog's bright color warns possible attackers.

Plants and animals that live in the canopy depend on each other. For example, there is a poison-dart frog from Panama that has a special relationship with plants called bromeliads (pronounced broh-MEE-lee-ads). Bromeliads grow high in the canopy on the branches of big trees. Their spiny leaves form a container that catches and holds water, making a tiny pond in the middle of the plant. After a mother frog's eggs hatch, she places each of her young in its own bromeliad pond. The mother frog returns every few days to feed her young. Meanwhile, their wastes are used by the bromeliads. This helps both the plants and the frogs.

The more scientists can understand canopy connections like this one, the better they can understand how tropical forests became so filled with life. They may also learn how to protect that life.

Charge!

Cecropia (pronounced si-KROW-pea-uh) trees (below left) are common in many tropical forests. They have huge, umbrella-like leaves. It's tempting to reach out and touch those big leaves, but people who do are usually greeted by a crowd of tiny, biting Azteca ants. The Azteca ants (below right) feed on a sugary substance produced by Cecropia plants and live in the plants' hollow stems.

In return, the ants help keep their trees safe and sound. They patrol leaves and branches, getting rid of leaf-eating insects. And if an animal disturbs the tree, they charge! The partnership between the ants and the trees is good for both insect and plant.

Do Birds Make a Difference?

Lots of forest insects eat leaves. This can weaken trees and slow their growth. But leaf-eating insects aren't the only animals in the canopy. Birds, frogs, and other insect-eaters live there, too. When a bird eats a leaf-eating insect, it ends the damage that insect can do. Scientist Sunshine Van Bael wants to know if birds help keep canopy trees healthy by eating insects. She thinks that if there were fewer birds in the canopy, there might be more insects to chew holes in tree leaves.

One way to find out is to keep birds from picking the insects from certain leaves. Sunshine did this by using sticks and netting to build a kind of cage that keeps birds out. She built the cages around tree branches. Insects can crawl through the netting to eat leaves. But birds are too big to get through, so they can't eat the insects.

Testing an Idea

Sunshine built net cages, like the one in the picture below, around canopy branches. It was hard to make ones that worked well. "Some were too heavy," remembers Sunshine, "and I had to redesign them."

To see if birds lower leaf damage by insects, Sunshine will compare leaves inside a net cage to leaves outside.

Just keeping birds away from certain leaves won't tell Sunshine if birds help keep the trees healthy. She needs to compare the damage insects do to leaves with and without birds. Each time she puts a net cage around a branch, Sunshine finds another branch near it. This branch does not get a net cage. It is a part of the experiment called a **control**. Sunshine compares what happens on the caged branches with what happens on the controls to find out if birds affect leaf damage.

So far Sunshine has measured more damage on leaves inside the net cages than on the controls. This makes her think that birds do help protect forest trees from insects. To be sure, she will collect information about birds, insects, and leaves for many months.

"I was really looking for a big-picture project," explains Sunshine. Seeing the big picture of how one group of animals affects the whole forest may help people understand how to preserve Earth's biodiversity. The health of tropical trees may depend partly on the biodiversity of insect-eating birds. If so, people in many parts of the world will need to work together to protect birds, because many birds travel great distances. Some birds live in tropical canopies for part of the year, but nest and raise their young in a completely different place.

(top)
Sunshine is holding a Royal Flycatcher. It's one of the birds that eat insects in the canopy.

(bottom)
Sunshine thinks the hardest part of her experiments is "learning to recognize all the different insects. There are so many up there."

41

Everybody's Important

Beetles play many roles in tropical forests. Beetles that eat plants can have a big effect on trees, vines, and other forest plants. Beetles that eat other insects help keep plant-eating insects under control. Beetles that eat plants and animals break down their food into tiny pieces. These pieces then return to the soil to be used again by plants. "Without those little animals, I don't think the forest can take care of itself," Elroy says. "It needs everybody. Small roles are still important."

Many people would like to preserve the biodiversity of tropical forests. But people also want to use these forests. Forest plants give us beautiful wood to build with, and nuts and fruit to eat. They provide the materials to make medicines, rubber, and other helpful items. People often destroy forests in order to use them. Perhaps canopy research can help people find ways to use forests and protect them at the same time.

The more scientists, such as (left to right) Sunshine Van Bael, Hector Barrios, Annette Aiello, and Elroy Charles, learn about tropical forests, the more they realize that everything is important. The forest needs beetles. It also needs the birds that eat beetles. It needs trees and vines and ferns. It needs all kinds of living things.

Glossary

biodiversity The variety of life in a certain location.

canopy The main top layer of a forest. The canopy can rise as tall as 60 meters (about 200 feet) above the forest floor.

chrysomelid [kris-o-MEL-id] A type of beetle also known as the leaf beetle.

classify In science, to group living things with other living things that share important characteristics.

control A mini-experiment that you do to make sure the data from the main experiment are correct.

dry tropical forest A tropical forest with a dry season and a rainy season.

emergent layer The layer of extra-tall trees that poke out above the canopy in a tropical forest. Some trees in this layer are as tall as a 15-story building.

entomologist [en-tuh-MOL-uh-jist] A scientist who studies insects.

equator An imaginary line that divides north and south on the globe.

gall A swelling in a leaf or stem, surrounding the egg of an insect. The swelling becomes a small "room," where the insect grows.

gall maker An insect that makes part of a plant swell, or grow larger.

gondola A small metal cage that hangs from the arm of a crane.

ground layer The bottom layer of a tropical forest. Herbs, ferns, and other small plants grow there.

larva A young insect.

leaf miner An insect that tunnels through the soft insides of leaves.

liana [lee-AH-na] A type of plant with a woody stem that clings to other plants.

rain forest A moist tropical forest that receives at least 2 meters (about 80 inches) of rain each year.

shrub layer The lowest part of a tropical forest, from the ground to about 5 meters (about 16 feet) above the ground. The area includes woody shrubs that can grow with little sunlight.

species A group of plants or animals able to mate with one another and give birth to young that can also mate and give birth.

taxonomist A scientist who is an expert in classifying living things.

tropical forest A forest near the equator, in the part of the world known as the tropics.

tropics Areas that lie near Earth's equator.

understory layer The layer in a tropical forest that is about 10 to 20 meters (about 33 to 66 feet) above the ground. The understory layer contains young canopy trees, small palms, and adult understory trees.

Further Reading

Clark, John, David Flint, Tony Hare, Keith Hare, and Clint Twist. *Encyclopedia of Our Earth.* New York, NY: Aladdin Books, 1995.

Fitzsimons, Cecilia. *Animal Habitats: Nature's Hidden Worlds.* Austin, TX: Raintree Steck-Vaughn, 1996.

Fredericks, Anthony D. *Exploring the Rain Forest: Science Activities for Kids.* Golden, CO: Fulcrum Publishing, 1996.

Lasky, Kathryn. *The Most Beautiful Roof in the World: Exploring the Rainforest Canopy.* San Diego, CA: Harcourt Brace, 1997.

Lye, Keith. *Equatorial Climates.* Austin, TX: Raintree Steck-Vaughn, 1997.

Patent, Dorothy Hinshaw. *Biodiversity.* New York, NY: Clarion Books, 1996.

Ross, Kathy. *Crafts for Kids Who Are Wild About Rainforests.* Brookfield, CT: Millbrook Press, 1997.

Savage, Steven. *Animals of the Rain Forest.* Austin, TX: Raintree Steck-Vaughn, 1997.

Index

Acknowledgments

Turnstone Publishing Group would like to thank Vibeke Horlyck for her review of this book, and Annette Aiello for her gracious support. The author wishes to also thank Georgina de Alba; Edwin Alberto Andrade; Olga Barrio; Hector Barrios; Yves Basset; Adriana Bilgray; Elroy Charles; the Doris family, Margaret, Charlie, Brendan, and Molly Doris-Pierce; Lindy Elkins, Jim Tanton, and Turner Bohlen; Eric Graham; Colonel Martha, Shoko Sake; Oscard Saldaña; Rita, Bob, Joel, and Gabriel Strachota; Sunshine Van Bael; Klaus Winter; and Joe Wright.

Credits:

Photographs courtesy of Chris Knight except for the following:

Annette Aiello: 24 second from the top, 34 bottom, 39 right inset; Animals, Animals/Kevin and Suzette Hanley: 38; Animals, Animals/Nigel J. H. Smith: 39 left; Beaufort, J. W., 1923, Courtesy of Natural History Museum: 12; Guerra, Marcos/STRI: 5 upper right silhouette, 6 top, 8 snake, 9 preying mantis, 17, 19 sloth and snake; Hawkins, Bradford A.: 24 top image and bottom three; Lowman, Dr. Margaret: 15 middle; Smithsonian Tropical Research Institute: 3 bottom, 6 bottom, 9 bromeliad, 16; Van Bael, Sunshine: 8 Royal flycatcher, 19 Royal Flycatcher, 40, 41, 42 left; Von Staden, Dietrich: 8 spider and katydid, 9 anteater, 19 anteater; Windsor, Donald: 25 main image and all silhouetted beetles on pages 2, 3, 4, 14, 20–21 except for largest insect on 20 left, 25, 30, 35, 38; Wittman, Philip K., 1996: 15 top and bottom.

Illustrations on pages 8–9 and 18 are by Patricia Wynne.

Illustrations on page 6 and 10 are by David Stevenson.

Illustrations on page 36 are courtesy of Annette Aiello.